WAYS OF ACHEIVING
SUCCESS DEPENDS ON
YOUR ABILITY

# THE GOOD IN
# PRODUCTIVITY

John L. Skeens

# TABLE OF CONTENT

A person needs to be determined for five primary reasons to succeed in life

1.  Being determined gives you the ability to keep trying until you succeed.

2. Persistence helps you overcome setbacks and difficulties

3. Being determined drives you to work hard and be persistent

4. Persistence fosters creativity and aids in problem-solving.

5.  Having determination helps you focus more clearly and work more efficiently.

CONCLUSION

# INTRODUCTION

In the world, there are many ways to succeed. However, when the majority of people hear the word "success," they immediately think of celebrities, artists, politicians, and businessmen.

They also think that if you follow their advice, you'll succeed, but this is wrong. They ignore the foundational elements of success, which are a person's dedication, perseverance, and drive to achieve their objectives. More importantly, people act by their interests rather than those of others. Successful people do what they love and what they think is best for their business.

The dictionary's definition of success is that it is the accomplishment of a purpose or objective. Thus, anyone can succeed as long as they achieve their aim or goal.

What damage might success have?
We all understand that achieving success involves making some sort of sacrifice. Success also has distinct requirements for you. But these sacrifices won't be in vain if you succeed in accomplishing your goal.

While many people undoubtedly achieve professional success, they frequently fall short of it on the emotional, social, and physical dimensions. The stress of falling behind in other areas causes them to come apart.

In some cases, a person's fixation with success makes other people uncomfortable around them. In other cases, they have even lost their minds. People can also become depressed if their definition of success differs from that of others. Thus, we could conclude that success has a lot of drawbacks.

Success and tenacity

It may seem unusual to some, but success takes a lot of work. Without it, success is impossible. It's not always necessary to work hard by performing arduous or physically demanding jobs. Maintaining a healthy physique, a keen mind, willpower, and a positive view of life are necessary for hard labor. And for all of those things, you need energy. Keep your mind at peace.

Along with that, venture outside of your comfort zone, take on challenging tasks, hone your skills, and most importantly, never stop learning. Make pleasant habits, surround yourself with nice people, and engage in physical and mental activity.

To sum it all up, we could say that success is like a seed that requires the right ratio of each element of life. Nobody can achieve success in life in a single day; it takes hard work and overcoming several challenges. The feeling of fulfillment you get after attaining your goal is mostly what defines success.

# CHAPTER ONE

# 10 Tips for Succeeding and Achieving Your Life Goals

Success is defined differently by each individual. Everyone strives for success, whether it be in the form of a fulfilling work, a beautiful home, or a happy family. Achieving your goals gives you a sense of accomplishment, motivates you to work hard, and shows that you have made a difference in a competitive world.

### We'll give you 10 success-related tips in this article.

Before defining success for yourself, you should make a list of what success entails for you and your family. Make a list of concrete steps you may take to ensure success after that.

## 1. Exhibit commitment

Being dedicated might provide you with the motivation you need to succeed. To begin the goal-setting process, make a list of the following things:

- How committed are you to the goal?
- What you're ready to do to achieve that goal
- Maintaining your dedication to your plan is crucial.

It's helpful to set aside at least 15 minutes each day for planning and reflection. You'll be able to stay on task and stay motivated if you do this.

Madisyn McKee, manager of social media and digital marketing, is aware of the elements that make success possible. Along with hiring new talent, she has launched efforts to support professional development. On success, she stated the following:

However, it's imperative to make sure you have realistic expectations for both the process and the outcome when gauging your commitment to your goal. If your perseverance doesn't bear fruit after a certain period, change your goal and take the necessary steps

1. Advice: Asking a friend or a family member for aid from time to time to help you maintain your commitments may be good. It keeps you focused on your goal to have someone to point out your shortcomings and celebrate your accomplishments.

2. Keep a travel journal: Instead of focusing only on the results of your work, think about the small steps

needed to succeed. Allowing yourself to enjoy small victories along the way can turn achieving your goal into a daily adventure and improve your chances of staying on track. By doing this, you'll learn interesting new things along the way that can aid in your personal growth.

3. Enjoy your journey: If anything takes too long to accomplish, it will be more difficult to succeed.

It's essential to keep your goals fun and pleasurable if you want to experience life emotionally well and go forward without losing perspective. It can be exciting and interesting to discover your potential.

4. Positivity: Having confidence in your abilities is the key to developing a positive mindset. It's essential to replace any negative thoughts with positive ones to keep going despite challenges in your way.

As you progress in your goals, you probably will pick up new abilities and form new ways of thinking. You won't succeed in achieving your goals right away. Because they will require effort and dedication to attain, it is imperative to have a positive mindset throughout the process.

5. Change your point of view: You might need to occasionally change your perspective to make a difficult situation better. Pretend that you are having a good day or a good week when in reality you are having a poor day or a bad week.

Observe how much your day or week changes after giving yourself the time and space to reflect on your situation while only using positive language. Your entire life might change if you carry on doing this for a while.

6. Tell the truth to yourself: If your goal isn't progressing, you might need to be brutally honest with yourself. Find a way to inspire yourself to achieve once you've come to an understanding.

Embrace stepping outside of your comfort zone. This could include adding another round of squats to your routine, approaching your supervisor about a promotion, or even signing up for a difficult college course you hadn't considered before.

7. **Remove all distractions:** Make a list of your life's time-wasters and distractions. This may be a stressful person, a phone call, a TV show, or even the environment. Now is the best moment to start changing your habits so that you can focus on success without becoming sidetracked. A few examples of eliminating distractions are as follows:

Put your phone in another room and turn it off when it's time to focus on your goal.

To switch off the TV, place the remote across the room.

Keep in touch with those who have a good impact on your life only.

8. **Have confidence in oneself:** To achieve your objectives, you cannot rely on other people. Your best friend is not permitted to take your place in a class. A promotion is not something you can get through your mother. Your partner cannot assist you in losing further weight. Each of these duties must be finished by you on your own. It may be beneficial to rely on others for emotional support, but remember that your friends and family also have needs that are distinct from your own. It's critical to hold yourself accountable for meeting your needs and attaining your goals.

9. **Keep with the plan:** Keep a schedule as you work toward your goals. In your calendar, write down targets for yourself like, "I will run a mile in seven minutes by the end of the month," or "I will save $5,000 by the end of the year."

Even if you don't finish the activity, you can still track your progress and keep track of where you started in your calendar. If you schedule and monitor your goals on a calendar, you will constantly have proof of your advancement. Having something tangible motivates perseverance in achieving success.

10. **Prevent exhaustion:** Keep your eyes on the prize, but make an effort not to let it overtake you. You'll maintain motivation without wearing yourself out if you make the process enjoyable while still reaching your objectives. You run the risk of burning out if you spend all of your time sitting idle and contemplating your objective.

Your once-fun objective could transform from something you anticipate completing into more of a job. Continue learning what you can accomplish and how far you can go to avoid burnout.

11. **Set SMART objectives:** You may track your development using the SMART approach and own your accomplishments.

## A manual for harnessing motivation to accomplish objectives

I'm John. He is getting ready to start the day on Monday morning. He begins working after oversleeping, rushing the kids to school, making their lunches, and almost forgetting to put on his pants. The realization that he had skipped his morning exercise

Our perspective differs. Maybe instead of ordering the third takeout this week, you had intended to start that book you've been meaning to read, tidy the house before your guests arrived, or get groceries.

Not enough hours is better In a day. However, it does. Finding 20 minutes to work out or do some cleaning is straightforward. In many cases, the true problem here is a lack of motivation. What chance do you have of achieving your objectives without it? Setting goals and being motivated has the ability of your achievement One influences the other. No matter how much you want to achieve a goal, taking the initial step may be difficult. This is crucial in terms of career objectives. To achieve your objectives, whether you want to establish a business, learn new skills, or write a book, you'll need motivation and self-control. Let's talk about how motivation enables people to accomplish their goals. You'll be one step closer to attaining your goals if you understand how they relate to one another.

**Give a reason**

Typically, you don't consider your incentive until it is no longer there. The next instant, you're in the zone and moving through your tasks rapidly. After that, you're exhausted, sleepy, and unable to focus. The mechanism that carries out a task or exhibits a behavior is the best way to define motivation. The motivation to finish what you've started comes from that emotion.

Every day, two common motivational styles affect you:

1.  Extrinsic motivation describes forces that push you in the direction of a particular goal. These could be advantageous, like a paycheck, or damaging, like the worry of being found out. If you imagine yourself in the shoes of a student, you should work toward getting a good grade rather than avoiding a failing grade.
2.  Internal motivators are referred to as intrinsic motivation. It's likely that you are pursuing this for your gain or because you have a deep passion for it.

Both can assist you in achieving your objectives, but they have different goals.

Short-term and long-term goals are considerably easier to achieve with the help of external motivators. Every time you accomplish a fitness objective or deliver a stellar presentation for the office, treat yourself. Long-term commitments call for intrinsic motivators.

If your heart isn't in it, starting a business might be challenging. You can use a variety of external motivators to keep up your productivity, but it can be difficult to retain your focus if there isn't inspiration to go along with your desire.

## Motivation in the workplace: Its significance

Your level of job happiness must be maintained, thus you must have the right motivation. Without it, you run the danger of losing employee engagement, which happened to 70% of the workers polled by Gallup. You won't ever be fully invested; all you'll do is go through the motions.

Over time, this could have several negative effects:

- More sleepiness and fatigue will set in.
- You face the danger of making a mistake and becoming more prone to stress.
- Your likelihood of burning out rises.
- Your health will deteriorate.
- The entire trip home will make you miserable.
- Even if it can appear that the labor you do has no purpose,

this is not always the case. There are other methods to keep motivated if your work or your coworkers don't inspire you. Self-motivation is crucial for this reason. It gives you the power to take control of your life, rediscover your purpose, and set your criteria of achievement. BetterUp can assist you in regaining your motivation. Our coaches will collaborate with you to determine your beliefs, choose practical goals, and maintain accountability.

# The connection between goals and inspiration

Even though having objectives makes you more motivated, you still need to be motivated to move in the right direction. This is a common illustration of the chicken-and-egg conundrum.

Choosing which comes first might be challenging. However, the problem is that neither of them does. In addition to motivation, you could also have a strong desire to set goals. It has also been demonstrated that failure to achieve a goal reduces motivation and self-esteem. Realistic goal-setting and achievement are essential for maintaining your brain's motivation and focus. How might setting goals work to increase motivation? By providing you with a concrete reward for your efforts, goals increase your motivation. You'll feel a sense of success after finishing each one, which will encourage you to keep going. It's critical to carefully set up your goals. You can become more motivated in the following ways by setting goals.

## 1. Set SMART objectives.

You have undoubtedly already heard of the SMART strategy if you have read anything about creating goals. These objectives are denoted by the acronym:

- What precisely are you attempting to achieve?What steps are you going to take?
- How able are you to measure your success?
- Can you achieve the objective with your current knowledge and resources?
- Relevance: Is this objective consistent with your larger purpose and core values?
- What time limit do you have?

Your personal and professional goals should adhere to this strategy. It will assist you in establishing reasonable goals for what you can accomplish, preventing disappointment and discouragement if you fall short of your goals. Even while failure is a fantastic teacher, the sensation of failure kills motivation more quickly than anything else. Businesswoman-writing-in-book-how-motivation-helps-in-achieving-goals

## 2. Begin modestly

Your list of accomplishments ought to look like a trail of breadcrumbs. Each one moves you closer to your main objective. It's crucial to prepare simple, first steps. You'll feel immediate progress once you do them, which will motivate you to keep going.

## 3. Monitor your development

When making and attaining objectives, it's simple to lose sight of your progress as you get into the swing of things. Create a system or download an app to periodically check your progress. As you advance, this will keep you motivated. It is helpful to use a visual representation, such as a checklist or a fundraising thermometer.

## 4. Give to yourself.

Setting and achieving objectives takes effort. You're likely driven to continue if you are consistent with your values and goals. However, it's crucial to add some flavor to give you energy on those difficult days.

How to spur yourself on to accomplish your objectives
Now that you understand how objectives can increase your motivation, a feedback loop will start to take shape. Your desire to complete the next one grows as you complete each one.

Your objectives will certainly get more challenging as you advance. Now the problem is to maintain the momentum. How to keep yourself inspired to continue:

Keep an appreciation notebook.
- Keep in mind the reasons you originally established your goals.
- Develop your resiliency
- Lean on your network of supporters
- Look for examples of success
- Imagine the future you desire.
- Keep a positive attitude

# CHAPTER TWO

# How does your mental condition impact your motivation levels?

Remember that your attitude determines your reality when you experience difficulty in your endeavors. For this reason, it's crucial to develop resilience. If you don't have grit and determination, you won't be able to overcome challenges without setting yourself up for failure.

The following psychological elements will influence your motivation:

- A spirit of defeat: You'll never succeed if you don't think you can accomplish your objectives.
- Self-critical thoughts: You're simply hurting yourself if you constantly criticize your actions.
- Unfilled needs: Every person has a hierarchy of needs, according to Maslow's pyramid. Your motivation will suffer if your needs are not being satisfied.
- Anxiety or depression: If you have been lacking motivation for longer than two weeks, you may have a long-term psychiatric illness. If you're worried about your mental health, think about talking to a mental health expert.

Thankfully, these psychological elements are reversible or, at the very least, manageable so that they don't significantly affect your day-to-day activities. To use them to your advantage, you might start by figuring out your particular motivators. This can help you feel better mentally

# How to recognize your motivational sources

Various motivators elicit various reactions from different people. Here are some queries to consider. Your responses will demonstrate what motivates you to succeed.

- Do you put forth more effort when a prize is on the line?
- Do you feel fulfillment in the accomplishment of your goals?
- Do you choose to be in charge of your work over maintaining the security of regular employment, even if it means giving it up?
- Do you strive to outdo your colleagues?
- Do you aspire to be an authority in your subject?
- Do you enjoy motivating people to achieve their goals?

You might place greater importance on some of these than others. Place them in this order. This will help your energy determines where your energy is focused When you are aware of your motivations, you may develop goals that are in line with them.

**External influences that may sap motivation**

Grit and perseverance are necessary to achieve your goals. And there will be numerous obstacles in your path that can prevent you from moving forward. Here are a few instances:

- Your organization's poor leadership
- Excessive workloads
- Workplace undervaluation Conflict with coworkers
- Job instability
- Undeveloped professional potential
- When you are going through these experiences.

it might be difficult to gauge their influence. However, as soon as you identify problems, you can take action to fix them.

# The significance of setting goals

Did you know that there is a straightforward procedure that can significantly boost our daily lives' effectiveness? With the help of this tool, we can make the most of each day, maximize our time, and enhance productivity. What is it, exactly? set objectives. That's correct; despite being so fundamental to living a successful life, this ability is frequently disregarded because of familiarity. People frequently forget the basic objective of goal setting since the concept becomes too familiar to them.

Objectives are.

## Describe goals.

A goal is described as what we want to accomplish through activity by any means.

## Annual, quarterly, and monthly big goals

The following goals will take a long time to complete. These goals typically have to do with things like money, health, owning a home, getting a new job, dating, etc. Thus, the main goals are outcome-oriented.

In other words, the focus is on a specific result, such as a business achieving $500,000 in profits in the third quarter, a person losing 20 pounds by the end of the year, or starting a relationship within six months. You see, they are objectives that must be set. However, attaining the major objectives on their own won't be beneficial. The following category of modest aims is what leads to the desired result.

## Simple Goals (Weekly and Daily)

Many minor elements go into achieving small goals.

After a big goal is determined, small goals must be made to achieve the big goal. As a result of processed objectives.

A process includes the steps that are used to achieve a goal. We stay motivated and accountable by setting daily and weekly goals.

If a careful strategy has been created, the minor aims will take care of the main aim. The beauty of it is that it eliminates any worry,If you trust the process and finish each of your tiny goals, the intended outcome will certainly be obtained.

Take the person who wishes to lose 20 pounds by the end of the year as an example.

Their weekly goals will look something like this:

- Spend five days a week at the gym.
- Eat healthfully six days a week this week.
- Take a daily stroll for 30 minutes.
- Avoid eating fast food the entire week.

After that, they would separate them into smaller, more doable daily goals:

- Spend an hour at the gym tomorrow.
- The weekly food planning will take place tomorrow.
- Go for a walk tomorrow after work.
- Meet with a personal trainer tomorrow.

You see, if a major goal is divided into smaller steps, the likelihood of success is much higher. Both big and little goals are important because they work best together. If a well-thought-out plan has been developed, the lesser aims will take care of the broader aim. The beauty of it is that it eliminates any worry. If you trust the process and finish each of your tiny goals, the intended outcome will certainly be obtained.

# CHAPTER THREE

# The real reason of motivation effort is the essence of success

Working hard is essential for success.

At least the majority of us desire to succeed in life. We aspire to succeed and improve as people. The key to success, though, can be summed up in just two words. BRUTAL WORK. Indeed, success and effort go hand in hand. Why? Because…

**"Hard work wins."**

Success and hard labor go hand in hand, and the former is the only way to get the latter. The difficulty with hard work is that it necessitates perseverance and dedication, which is a problem for many. But to succeed, we must put in the time and be prepared to believe in the process. There is no getting around this reality.

The good news is that few individuals are willing to work extremely hard, which is beneficial for you. Most people tend to gravitate toward convenience, comfort, and stability. especially when they feel their careers or businesses are stagnant or that they don't appreciate their work. Most people soon cease caring and gradually limit their actions to only those that are required. Without a sure, this is a disaster for those who would downplay the importance of perseverance. However, it is a chance for you and everyone else who is prepared to put in the tough effort. Indeed, hard labor is not enjoyable or convenient, but success without it is essentially unachievable. With being said, continue reading if you're interested in finding out why perseverance is essential for success as well as a few steps you can take to truly embrace perseverance and make it work for you.

**Work hard to succeed; never wish for it.**

You are continually investing in your future success as you put effort into your goals each day, and over time, you will start to see the progress you have made. You will be motivated to continue moving forward as you start to see your progress and realize that if you stay on this course, you will eventually arrive where you want to be. As your job progresses, you'll start to feel a sense of pride and success that will motivate you to keep going. But to succeed, we must put in the time and be prepared to believe in the process. There is no getting around this reality. The good news is that few individuals are willing to work extremely hard, which is beneficial for you. Most people tend to gravitate toward convenience, comfort, and stability. especially when they feel their careers or businesses are stagnant or that they don't appreciate their work.

# Why Struggle Is The Secret To Success

Success and hard work both need a lot of time and effort, which is the thing about both. For success to progressively increase over time, you must put in a lot of effort. Therefore, you must choose whether you want to put up with the discomfort of hardship and enjoy the benefits, or look back and regret never having tried. Having said that, here are some things to think about before you choose.

### 1. There Are Prices For Everything

For the vast majority of people, achieving success costs money. Hard work goes into that charge. People who have achieved varying levels of success in their lives are aware that hard work and sacrifice are necessary to succeed. Even when you don't feel like going to work, you have to get up early and go. You must overcome the challenges and keep the end in sight, understanding that each step you take will get you closer to accomplishing it.

### 2. You Can Make Your Luck Through Hard Work

You are probably just a spectator waiting for something to happen or fall into your lap if you are an average Joe and just coast through life. The likelihood of this happening is improbable, in actuality. Goals, desires, and ambitions are necessary, but you also need to have the motivation to carry them through. Success does not come easily, but with the correct amount of tenacity and effort, one's chances of success increase. Don't let opportunities pass you by when they come your way; seize them.

### 3. Working hard helps you form values

Other things start to happen when you adopt a hard worker's mentality. Where others might give up because it was too difficult for them, you begin to persevere. Although you start to appreciate what you already have, you'll still be working hard to make sure bigger things happen. But most importantly, you stop blaming other people for your problems and start looking for solutions. Both being lazy and procrastinating are put to an end. Time is of importance, you realize, and these things were preventing you from moving forward. Additionally, you start to feel less insecure, and your dread of failing lessens.

### 4. Work Ethic Promotes Discipline

Even the most motivated individuals may experience days when they feel like giving up and throwing up the towel, but that is when discipline comes into play. It won't always be simple. No matter how difficult the task seems, discipline makes sure you still wake up and face the day. You always provide your best effort, and you're motivated to get the desired outcome. As time goes on, you'll become more aware of the amount of time and energy you've already put into pursuing your goals. You'll come to understand that what you gave up to get where you are is not worth losing up on since you've already made too much progress.

## 5. You Get What You Give

If you invest money consistently over time, it will ultimately start to accumulate and you will have a sizable portfolio. The same is true of hard effort; you get back what you put in. You are continually investing in your future success as you put effort into your goals each day, and over time, you will start to see the progress you have made. You will be motivated to continue moving forward as you start to see your progress and realize that if you stay on this course, you will eventually arrive where you want to be. As your job progresses, you'll start to feel a sense of pride and success that will motivate you to keep going.

# Things to Pay Attention To To Maximize Your Hard Work

**how to exert effort**

You will surely develop in life through hard work, thus it's important to fight off vices like procrastination, excuses, and sloth. To make sure that you realize your potential, you must do other things in addition to working hard.

## 1. Work Cleverly

There are many people out there who work long hours but earn little money or succeed in their objectives. This is probably a result of their lack of education and expertise, which would allow them to make greater use of their efforts. You must always be learning if you want to advance in your career. Work hard at your job, but also make sure you're working hard to learn more and come up with ideas that will offer you a competitive edge.

## 2. Generate Chances

Many people today have a good education and are knowledgeable about their fields. They don't have the opportunities, nevertheless, to advance.

To influence people to want to give you opportunities in this situation, you must put a lot of effort into your networking and people skills. Adopting the hard work ethic means working hard to develop your soft skills and your capacity for action, as well as working hard to increase your physical fitness. You will have a lot more opportunities if you do this. Work hard to develop the talents that will provide you with more opportunities.

### 3. Make a Success Plan

You must make preparations to guarantee your success if you want your efforts to be successful. Learn everything you can about your industry, keep looking for new chances and collaborations, and then establish strategies for how you can use that knowledge to take advantage of those opportunities. Without a plan, your efforts will nevertheless provide some results. However, if you add sound planning to the mix, you can significantly cut down on the time and work needed to reach your objectives.

### 4. Overcome Your Fears

In our endeavors, we will confront many difficulties, but one of the biggest is dread, particularly fear of the future. Learn to overcome your aversions and accept that things like failure are only a part of what will help you develop into a better version of yourself rather than trying to ignore it. You will impede your advancement if you are willing to put in a lot of effort but are hesitant to take advantage of certain opportunities because you lack confidence or are afraid of failing. Therefore, put a lot of effort into overcoming your fear so that you can overcome the anxiety-inducing challenges with much more ease.

### 5. Develop Your Self-Belief

The disease of self-doubt is one thing that frequently prevents people from working hard and succeeding.

Your actions are likely to take this form if you consistently think that your efforts will be in vain. Similar to this, you won't be as likely to do your finest work if you have any uncertainty that your efforts will be fruitless. Additionally, your efforts will be hampered if you don't believe that you deserve the results of your labor because you lack confidence in yourself. Instead, recognize your skills and fight to overcome your limitations to build confidence in both yourself and your job. You'll work harder the more assured and self-assured you become.

Whether we like it or not, we all have to put in work to pay the bills. However, some people will go above and beyond this and push harder than others to succeed. Yes, work is not always enjoyable, but regardless of the industry we are in, it is the only way we can advance.

So keep in mind that success comes from hard work. Your chances of developing to take advantage of the enormous opportunities that are sure to present themselves increase the harder you work at your career, business, or creative endeavors, the more eager you are to take on new challenges, and the more diligently you try to learn new things. **Working Hard Pays Off in Success** Once you've attained the achievement you were chasing, you won't look back on how hard you worked. However, you will undoubtedly do so if you just relax, take it easy, and let life pass you by. Aim high and put in your all because success comes from working hard.

Until you accomplish your goals,

# Benefits of Setting Goals

Why do we need to start by setting goals? It is a question that merits an answer because there should never be an instance in life when something is done without a good reason. Objectives are useful because they provide direction and purpose. When we make goals for ourselves, we offer ourselves something to strive for. Holding onto that result leads to a more ordered and purposeful life. Many excellent attributes are fostered by setting goals. Once a goal has been determined, motivation is needed to continue working toward it every day. Action must also be given attention.

Setting objectives for ourselves can help us live more purposeful and productive lives. Without a clear objective, creating a plan can be difficult. Without a plan, we'll probably be less successful as well.

## Any goal is attainable!

This is one of the most charming aspects of goal setting. Contrary to popular belief, a goal does not necessarily need to be large to be set. Any part of our lives can benefit from setting goals.

Setting goals considerably improves our chances of success. Because setting goals promotes focus, structure, and direction. No matter how big or small, daily or monthly, the goals are all equally important. When we have a clear plan for life, the chances that we will achieve our objectives are higher. Additionally, it might lead to a more fulfilling existence.

In my experience, having goals helps me feel more content and productive. My overarching goals guide the everyday tasks I want to finish. Nothing makes me feel more accomplished than looking over my list at the end of the day to see everything I was able to accomplish. Setting goals has immense value, and the benefits that follow are equally significant.

## Benefits of Goal Setting

Now that we are aware of what goal setting is and its advantages. But what about the benefits of the method?

As would be expected, setting goals has several benefits. Here are a few examples:

## Encourages Motivation

Goals increase our motivation in two separate ways. They start by giving us something to aim for. We are more motivated to work toward a goal when we have one.

Second, no matter how big or little the goal, the closer we get to it, the more motivated we become. The satisfaction we get after achieving a goal motivates us to do it repeatedly, which is the cause of this.

## makes one more responsible

We must assume personal responsibility for our lives if we want to flourish and live in general welfare. We give ourselves something to work toward by setting goals. Because we set the goal, we are responsible for achieving it by our actions. We are aware of what must be done to accomplish our goals. We alone are responsible for whether or not the everyday tasks that must be accomplished are carried out. It is tremendously empowering and freeing to be in control of your life.

"Our success and general well-being depend on us not having control over our life. We give ourselves something to work toward by setting goals. Because we set the goal, we are responsible for achieving it by our actions.

## You Can Monitor Your Development

This is especially true for minor objectives. I've found that whenever I just set a big goal, I often end up abandoning up because I get discouraged along the way.

This happens because it is impossible to recognize every little improvement made along the way. By setting little goals, we can keep track of all the work we've completed. Even if we just make small forward progress at a time, this will help keep us inspired and on track to accomplish the broader goal.

## Identifies Your Priorities

Setting priorities is crucial if we are to accomplish anything in life. You must establish priorities for yourself to prevent getting distracted. To do that, setting goals is a terrific idea. When we set a major goal and then multiple smaller ones, some priorities become obvious. For example, prioritizing exercise is essential whether you want to shed weight or build muscle. Similar to this, if our goal is to increase our income, then making more money must come first. Setting goals helps us swiftly decide what will be our top priorities. Setting goals is important, and it is easy to see why when you consider these four benefits. The current problem is how to go about goal setting. Even though it sounds like a pretty simple idea, having a set of guidelines is typically beneficial.

We require SMART objectives because they must be precise, measurable, reachable, pertinent, and time-bound.

# Setting smart Goals: A Guide

The process of setting goals is much easier when there are rules to follow. That is the greatest likelihood of success.

There is a collection of best practices for setting goals that goes by the abbreviation SMART. It works well for both major and minor objectives. So let's begin with the first principle, which is specific, and then go over the meaning of the phrase.

## Specific

The goals should be distinct and definite. If they are, getting there won't be simple for you. Because of this, making SMART goals requires that they be specific. We've already discussed how having high goals might result in achieving lesser ones. If the big goal is not stated, choosing the daily targets will be much more difficult.

Before deciding on a certain objective, there are five questions you should ask yourself.

- What do I want?
- Why is achieving the goal so important?
- Who is involved in the process I use to achieve my goals?
- What resources are needed?
- What challenges prevent me from completing the task?

Once you learn the answers to these five questions, you will have a very clear idea of your goal. This helps you have a clear mental image of what you are striving to do.

Objectives shouldn't be overly vague. If they are, getting there won't be simple for you. Because of this, making SMART goals requires that they be specific.

## Measurable

A goal needs to be measurable, according to the third requirement for goal-setting. Here, it is addressed how to recognize when a goal has been reached. For instance, if your goal is to increase your revenue, you cannot just make the target larger. How can you ever know if it was successful if that's all it takes? Even if a $10 increase in sales is significant, I doubt that's what you're hoping for. So, a measurable goal for the coming year would be to increase your revenue by $10,000. By doing this, you will have a clear objective to strive for and it will be simple to recognize when it has been reached.

## Achievable

Making sure a goal is attainable is one of the most challenging aspects of SMART objectives. Never undersell yourself by not taking on a difficult task. For lack of a better phrase, setting an unattainable goal may nevertheless lead to frustration and ultimately giving up. To avoid this, it is preferable to set ambitious yet attainable goals. These reachable objectives can eventually pave the way for more ambitious goals that were formerly thought to be unattainable. This is one of the wonderful things about objectives. What currently seems unachievable may turn out to be well within your capability in a few years if the goals set in front of it were realistic for you at the time.

## Relevant

The fourth condition for goal formulation is that a goal must be relevant. Simply said, when a goal is in line with your values and matters to you, it is relevant. This holds for both lofty and modest goals.

You can decide if your goal is pertinent by asking yourself the following questions:

- Is this really what I want?
- Does it make sense for me to have a goal?
- Do my values match the outcome?
- Are my daily goals consistent with my overall goal?

## Limited in time

The final topic to be covered is the section on time in the SMART guidelines. There must be a deadline by which each of our goals will be accomplished. The time frame gives us a sense of urgency. When we decide when a goal will be completed and set a deadline for its accomplishment, our priorities are established. This will help to keep us on track and focused on achieving our aims. If a goal is not time-bound, it will likely be dropped. Become only a wish rather than an objective to be pursued.

## Final Thoughts

We establish objectives to direct our behavior toward getting the outcomes we want. These objectives provide us with focus, clarity, direction, and a sense of meaning in life. We can set greater goals in addition to daily and weekly ones. The benefits of this practice include an increase in motivation, a better sense of responsibility, measuring progress, and support with determining priorities.

When setting goals, the SMART criteria make for an excellent template. Make sure they are specific, measurable, time-bound, relevant, and reachable. The goals you have set for yourself will then be solid and clear.

# CHAPTER FOUR

# A person needs to be determined for five primary reasons to succeed in life.

Determined people are more likely to overcome challenges and reach their objectives. The ability to keep going in the face of obstacles and setbacks while working toward a goal demonstrates determination. Persistent people can develop their skills, learn from their errors, and overcome obstacles. Success also requires tenacity, which motivates people to work for their obobjectives

## 1. Being determined gives you the ability to keep trying until you succeed.

Tion, you'll give up earlier than you think. With resolution, you can persevere and persist until you reach your goal.

At the age of 65, Harland Sanders was broke and without money. He was forced to close his business after a new road was built around his restaurant. Harland was struggling, but he was still determined to fight his way back. But all he had was his special fried chicken recipe. Then Harland started on his mission to get business owners to try his top-secret fried chicken recipe. He visited every restaurant in his neighborhood, going door to door. Numerous nights were spent by him sleeping in his automobile. He even approached restaurant owners and had his fried chicken prepared there and then. You probably know what transpired next. Before his fried chicken recipe was accepted, Harland Sanders had his 1,009th rejection. Colonel Harland Sanders had 600 businesses selling his recognizable chicken by the year 1964. The way we eat has changed because of that one yes.

The most well-known accomplishment of Colonel Harland Sanders is the creation of Kentucky Fried Chicken or KFC. Colonel Harland Sanders would never succeed if he lacked tenacity. Despite all the odds, he was able to persist and endure because of his tenacity. Know more about it by reading below After being rejected a few times, the majority of people would have given up. not Colonel Sanders, though. He was adamant. And that's how he was able to endure so many rejections while continuing to advance.

So, do you possess the same tenacity as Colonel Harland Sanders?

## 2. Persistence helps you overcome setbacks and difficulties

The ability to overcome failures, setbacks, and difficulties along the way is the second reason why determination is crucial. It's hard to succeed, let's face it. It is tough. Everyone would be successful if it were simple. Additionally, because success is challenging, you will encounter numerous obstacles and disappointments along the road. As a result, without perseverance, you will never reach the goal.

Extraordinary people vary from those who are ordinary because they are driven. They are persistent and will go the "extra" mile. Because of this, they are 'extraordinary. The average person, on the other hand, decides to give up and resign anytime they experience failures and setbacks. They opt for the simple solution.

This explains why so many individuals have ambitions and objectives, yet only a small percentage of them are successful in making their aspirations come true.

What if your aim is to become a popular YouTuber? You intend to release two videos each week. You have eight videos published two months later, yet your channel has less than 100 subscribers. What do you think?

That's bad, right? And here is where the majority of folks decide to give up. Your level of resolve also matters a lot in this situation.

Building a successful YouTube channel is a goal that someone truly committed to it would never give up on.

Those who lack tenacity, however, will give up on their objective. They'll decide to be in a different direction. They will also make shoddy explanations for why they won't be able to attend.

## 3. Being determined drives you to work hard and be persistent

Yes, those who are determined are willing to put in a lot of effort to get what they want. However, those who lack motivation will opt to remain in their familiar surroundings and resist change. Look at how hard you work to achieve your goal to determine how determined you are. Your behavior speaks volumes. People who lack determination will only work toward their objectives when it is convenient. Only when they are inspired will they decide to go after their goals and take action.

But those who are committed will persevere regardless of the circumstances, regardless of how they feel.

Do you know that at midnight, Tiger Woods trained outside in the rain? He said, "It doesn't rain very often in Northern California," when his friend asked him why he was striking golf balls at three in the morning. I can only practice striking in the rain at this time. The story can be found here. And for that reason, Tiger Woods rose to prominence as one of the game's top players. He was adamant about reaching the top and committed to doing so. As you can see, you become persistent when you are motivated to do something or to reach a goal. You are prepared to put your all into making it happen.

Being determined forces you to put forth a lot of effort. You gain the power and fortitude necessary to overcome all obstacles and take decisive action.

So, are you adamant about achieving your objectives no matter what?

# 4. Persistence fosters creativity and aids in problem-solving.

There is always a way when there is more zeal. It doesn't matter if you can succeed; what matters is how determined you are to do so. Success is a function of why something is done, not how it is done. Many people make the mistake of believing that their inability to achieve is due to a lack of skill, knowledge, or talent. However, your success will not be determined by your expertise, knowledge, or talents. It depends on your resolve, persistence, and strength of will. You see, nobody is a master by birth. Every master started as a novice. And that implies that you can develop your skills in anything. If you believe that success comes from talent or skill, you need to reevaluate your assumptions.

Do you know that Soichiro Honda's factory suffered two bombings as a result of the war, and a third time as a result of an earthquake? Honda, though, was committed to succeeding. That's how he came up with the concept of adding an engine to a bicycle, and the Honda Super Cub was the result. The rest became history. Following the release of her Harry Potter books, J.K. Rowling became the first author to earn a billion dollars. She didn't have a lucky start, though. Rowling was unemployed, divorced, and penniless. She was dependent on government assistance. But she persisted in writing till she realized her ambition because she was tenacious.

The legendary co-founder of Apple, Steve Jobs, was let go from the business he built. But he was tenacious and enthusiastic about his work. He then founded NeXT, a new business, and acquired Pixar. After that, Apple acquired NeXT, and Jobs returned to the company as CEO. He later introduced the iPod, iPad, and iPhone, which completely changed the mobile and tech industries.

The more you read famous people's lives, the more you'll realize how important determination is in achieving achievement.

If you're committed, you'll figure something out. And if a solution is not available, you will invent one!

So, do you intend to be successful? If you do, a solution will be found.

## 5. Having determination helps you focus more clearly and work more efficiently.

The road to success is not easy. And on your trip, things will undoubtedly go wrong. There will inevitably be errors, failures, and setbacks. However, if you are resolute, you may continue to be motivated and focused even when things don't go as planned. One of the most significant advantages of independence is that. It enables you to maintain concentration even when circumstances are not favorable. People's sentiments and emotions frequently have an impact on them. When you purchase a stock and the market experiences a sell-off, you will be impacted and tempted to do the same.

# CONCLUSION

**10 Conduct Patterns That Will Derail Your Success**

- When you deal with executives and business leaders for decades, you really can't help but see what endures and what doesn't.
- One thing I've found is that success is not determined by your inherent qualities or personal habits. It is your actions.
- Take a deep, honest look in the mirror and see if any of these career-limiting tendencies apply to you if you want to succeed in the long run.
- Residing in the past or the future. While it's true that we can learn from the past, concentrating on it causes harm to oneself.
- Similar to this, you can make plans and have goals for the future, but if your actions aren't centered on the here and now, you'll never come true.
- Jokingly uninterested. The words "whatever works," "it's all good," and "no worries" are frequently used in today's society, but you hardly ever hear them from those who have achieved great success.
- Apathetic is not one of the many things they might be.
- Oversensitivity. You're going to struggle in the real business world if you have such a thin skin that any criticism drives you mad and every little thing offends you.

- Business executives typically possess a sense of humor and humility for a reason. It's kind of a prerequisite. Don't be so serious with yourself.
- One final point. You have at least two or three problems to address if any of this offends you to the point where you want to post an incensed flame reply.

Alternatively, consider the positive aspect. At least you aren't apathetic.

www.ingramcontent.com/pod-product-compliance
Lightning Source LLC
Chambersburg PA
CBHW062300290526
45794CB00006B/2634